Contemporary Mexican Architecture

Continuing the Heritage of Luis Barragán

Contemporary Mexican Architecture

Continuing the Heritage of Luis Barragán

Sandy Baum

Schiffer Publishing Ltd

4880 Lower Valley Road • Atglen, PA 19310

Published by Schiffer Publishing, Ltd.
4880 Lower Valley Road
Atglen, PA 19310
Phone: (610) 593-1777; Fax: (610) 593-2002
E-mail: Info@schifferbooks.com

For our complete selection of fine books on this and related subjects, please visit our website at www.schifferbooks.com. You may also write for a free catalog.

This book may be purchased from the publisher. Please try your bookstore first.

We are always looking for people to write books on new and related subjects. If you have an idea for a book, please contact us at proposals@schifferbooks.com Schiffer Publishing's titles are available at special discounts for bulk purchases for sales promotions or premiums. Special editions, including personalized covers, corporate imprints, and excerpts can be created in large quantities for special needs. For more information, contact the publisher.

Other Schiffer Books by the Author:
Colores: *Mexican Interiors.* ISBN: 978-0-7643-3301-9. $29.99
Mexican Gardens & Patios. ISBN: 978-0-7643-3267-8. $29.99
San Miguel's Mexican Exteriors. ISBN: 978-0-7643-3004-9. $39.99
San Miguel's Mexican Interiors. ISBN: 978-0-7643-2947-0. $14.95
The William Spratling Legacy. ISBN: 978-0-7643-3886-1. $49.99
Hammered Copper. ISBN: 978-0-7643-352-0. $29.99

Other Schiffer Books on Related Subjects:
Igloo: *Contemporary Vernacular Architecture.* Alejandro Bahamón & Ana Cañizares. ISBN: 978-0-7643-4192-2. $29.99
The Art of Brazilian Architecture. Joaquim Nabuco. ISBN: 978-0-7643-4066-6. $60.00

Designed by RoS
Type set in Helvetica Neue

ISBN: 978-0-7643-4602-6
Printed in China

Contents

Luis Barragán, Architect
Casa Gonxalex Luna, 1928
Guadalajara, Jalisco

Preface

When I started working on this book, I thought I would be able to just sit back and solicit the Mexican architects with an "Invitation to Participate" via email. That started off working just fine. However, after getting mixed reactions, some slower than others, I decided to take this "Invitation to Participate" on the road. In so doing, I traveled to several Mexican cities, including Guadalajara, Monterrey, and Mexico City, where I met with architects who impressed me with their commitment to their profession, a reaction I was not getting communicating through the emails. Architects who looked to me as if they were still in high school proved to be professors in the universities where they were giving back to their profession. I was also impressed with the quality of design I was seeing, design, I realized, that would stand up to much of the world design I had been exposed to up until now.

Mexico's contemporary architecture got its awakening through the eyes of Luis Barragán, one of Mexico's most influential twentieth century architects.

> Barragán changed Mexico's architecture into a vibrant, sensuous Mexican aesthetic by adding vivid colors and textural contrasts and accentuating his buildings with natural surroundings. He once said that light and water were his favorite themes. (Design Museum)

Many of the architects I interviewed, when asked which architect(s) had an influence on their career, paid homage to Barragán, along with a few other well-known architects of the twentieth century—Le Corbusier, Mies van der Rohe, Frank Lloyd Wright, and Philip Johnson, to name a few.

> While the country remains deeply conservative and religious, a new class of affluent, urban Mexican architects has emerged, who are beginning to achieve success not only throughout Mexico, but for clients from around the globe who are inviting Mexico's architects to bring their design talent to foreign soils, such as Japan, Dubai, Europe, China, and the United States.
> —The Plan: Architecture & Technologies in Detail

The contemporary Mexican architect is having an impact on the world scene with a younger generation of Mexican architects bringing a new level of inventiveness to Mexico, responding creatively to the social needs of their country with a wealth of fresh thinking to reinvigorate the profession in this former third world country.

When I visited the architects, I came away in awe of and deeply appreciative for what they are achieving today—innovation and an explosion of design talent.

This book showcases 26 Mexican architects' contemporary design in a wide variety of interior and exterior spaces. Each architect's work is featured in a dedicated chapter with large full-color photography capturing their latest design. An Architect Directory follows the last architect featured in the back of this book. The photographs included in each architect's chapter were supplied by that architect's office and were taken either by a staff photographer in the office or an outside professional photographer. A list of the professional photographers and the photos, with which they are credited, can also be found in the Photographer Index in the back of the book. This author took the first eight photographs, which are residential details designed by two of the more influential architects of the twentieth century in Guadalajara, Luis Barragán and Pedro Castellanos Lambley.

> We seek out the aspirations of a place, trying to bring them to their next stage of evolution, where the new structure respectfully talks of the past, is firmly rooted in the present and gives a sense of direction for the future.
>
> —Hierve

In the Introduction, I have asked three architects, one from each of the major cities of Mexico City, Guadalajara, and Monterrey to give their take on the state of contemporary Mexican architecture and where Mexico's architects fit into the global scheme of things. I think you will find their commentary interesting.

—Sandy Baum

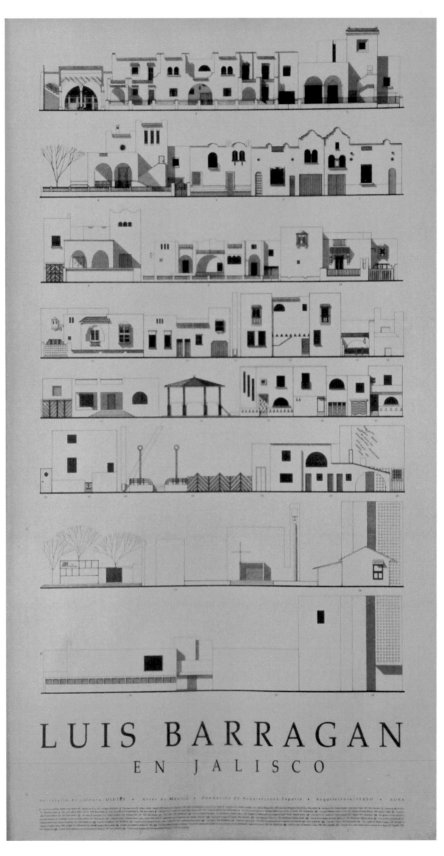

Poster
Luis Barragán, Architect
Guadalajara, Jalisco

Luis Barragán, Architect
Casa Gonxalex Luna, 1928
Guadalajara, Jalisco

Mexico opened its borders at the end of the 1980s, but it was not until the last decade of the twentieth century that new imported materials and construction systems were introduced. The culture of the last century created the foundation and established the conditions for advancement, but opening the frontier created an endless flow of possibilities for Mexican architects, with all their strength, to affirm their place in the twenty-first century. Today everything is consolidated— internationally, historically, and tecnologically—shaping our task, which rises according to the new requests of our clients.

Globalization has had a profound impact. In the past fifteen years, we have seen the migration of architects to the best universities and architectural firms in the world. Joint ventures have been undertaken, with national and foreign architectural firms participating in international competitions and collaborating on projects in our country and abroad. These are clear signs of the expansion of globalization in the good sense—the one we live in.

The fast pace of development in Mexico has created another reality that shapes our architecture. The need to be up-to-date forces projects and construction to be presented to the public hastily and, in the majority of cases, without the budgets required to fully realize them. Still, the objectives are fulfilled: the

Introduction — Three Participating Architects

Contemporary Mexican Architecture

—Juan Pablo Serrano Orozco, Mexico City
Fellow of the Mexican National Academy of Architecture

With the ease of travel and communication between nations and cities, society in the second decade of the twenty-first century is global. This international influence has modified the classic patterns of Mexican architecture—the pre-Hispanic with its open spaces, the colonial, the vernacular, the Arab inheritance, modernism, and the styles of the nineteenth and twentieth centuries—and resulted in Contemporary Mexican Architecture.

As in the rest of the world, new materials and constructions systems are having a major impact on architecture in Mexico. Today's projects are being shaped by the ebb and flow of global and regional trends, as well as by developments in hand labor and technology. Without abandoning the heritage of the millenarian constructors and the excellence of the artisanal work that makes it rich and complete, Contemporary Mexican Architecture is global and the equal of any other in the world.

image is refreshed, updated, and avant-garde. The revolution is not exclusive to architecture; it can also be seen in gastronomy and design, which are suffering the same phenomenon. It is simply the result of the sophistication and demands of the lifestyle of our times.

Architectural design is found at restaurants, beauty parlors, VIP lounges, clubs, offices, as well as in housing, urban infrastructure, hotels, industry, and the commercial fields. Society demands and consumes fresh and current design. This is the present reality in our country and economy, and is a phenomenon that is especially visible in the main cities of Mexico. Twenty years ago there were three major cities in Mexico. Now it has more than twenty-five modern, global, and cosmopolitan metropolises that are still growing and in need of contemporary design.

Contemporary Mexican Architecture is flourishing and in a state of continuous transformation, thanks to the big changes generated in the commercial, cultural, and social fields. But what is most important is that all this transformation has started to focus on the main feature of architecture: people, who live, use, and give architecture its true value.

Mexican contemporary architecture is a process, from the people to the people.

Contemporary Architecture in Mexico:
A Melting Pot of
Cultural Heritages

—Juan Carlos Name Sierra, Guadalajara
*Academic-Emeritus, Mexican National
Academy of Architecture*

Contemporary Mexican architecture is the result of a cultural process stretching back to 1200 BC, when Mesoamerican cultures became sedentary and began producing their first permanent architectural works. The height of this period can be placed between 200 BC and 1500 AD, when the grand odificos whose ruins we see today (and that belong to World Heritage listings) were built.

After the Spanish Conquest, the colonial New Spain cities were planned and established, as one might expect, following European urban and architectural patterns. However, even these "new" developments were already adapted and localized to each community, contributing since then to the style and particular identity of Mexican architecture.

The country's architectural style continued to evolve under these same premises until the dawn of the twentieth century, when new socioeconomic circumstances, added to the arrival of new materials and construction techniques and the continued influence of European and now also North American design styles contributed to the shaping of the Mexican architect.

The National School of Architecture can trace its origins to the colonial Academy of San Carlos, the first architectural school in the Americas, founded over 230 years ago in Mexico City. This prestigious institution prepared some of the most renown Mexican architects, who in turn contributed to the creation of highly reputed architectural schools and colleges in public and private universities, cradles of the present contemporary Mexican architecture creators.

Nowadays, with globalized ease-of-access to materials and construction techniques from anywhere in the world, it has certainly become more difficult to create a pure "regional" architectural style, but even in the twenty-first century, a few Mexican design programs maintain the use of specific idiosyncratic elements that have transcended time. Some examples in the modern Mexican house include the use of a portico or a central courtyard, the option for large, unopened walls, and, overall, the fantastic utilization of color.

Luis Barragán, Architect,
Casa Franco—1929,
Guadalajara, Jalisco

The Guadalajara-born Luis Barragán, the 1980 Pritzker Prize recipient, is a clear example of creative work influenced by the vernacular architecture of Jalisco, the Mexican haciendas, and also the Spanish and North African styles. Yet Barragán's style was an entirely new product, bound to become a staple of later twentieth century architecture, and a global influence in this art form.

Mexican architects have grown under impressive cultural baggage; their work has traces of every architectural tradition they have been exposed to, and the influence of Pre-Columbian, Colonial, European (and in the case of Spain, also its Moorish past), and, closer to home, North American architecture and design styles are clearly noticeable. However, contemporary Mexican creators have developed and are currently developing high quality works that are, as in Barragán's case, the result of a proper mixture of these influences, an amalgamation that has managed to come up with a very particular, well-defined, highly recognizable, and highly regarded style.

Luis Barragán, Architect,
Casa Franco—1929,
Guadalajara, Jalisco

Monterrey´s Architectural Journey into the Twenty-first Century

—Gilberto L. Rodriguez, Monterrey
ITESM / Harvard University
Graduate School of Design

Monterrey, the Mexican northern city known as the industrial capital of the country, with such important companies as the cement giant CEMEX or the Cuahutemoc-Moctezuma brewery (both founded more than a century ago), has always been an example to all of Mexico, with its hard-working community and its visionary leaders.

It was in the last decade of the nineteenth century that Monterrey became one of the most important cities in the country, due to a tax break strategy created in order to attract investments and industrialize the city. From that point, Monterrey gave birth to most of its main companies and started an era of great productivity and economic growth. Later, in the early 1940s, a private university, The "Instituto Tecnológico y de Estudios Superiores de Monterrey" (ITESM) was founded with the main goal of educating engineers and technicians for the city´s growing factories. Another important architecture school that was founded in the same decade was the UANL, which has remained until today as the largest in the city.

Unfortunately, they were both architecture schools mostly oriented towards efficient and economic building, without a true vision of architecture as a cultural expression or a form of art. For this reason, the city was, in fact, during most of the twentieth century, a place with a lack of character, without a true architectural identity, except for some very good—but also quite scarce—examples. Some of these significant buildings were created by renowned local architects, such as Guillermo Gonzalez, Ricardo Guajardo, or Ramón Lamadrid—or in more recent times by Eduardo Padilla and Adan Lozano, just to name a few, together with Oscar Bulnes, another significant architect who got the commission of designing the "Macroplaza," a large scale downtown renovation project built during the eighties.

Monterrey, however, has always had a certain presence, a number of nationally renowned architects working on its territory, and one of them was precisely the one who did the "ITESM" campus: Enrique de la Mora y Palomar, who had previously built "La Purisima," the first modern church in all of The Americas, in our city in 1946. De la Mora, born in Guadalajara but who practiced in Mexico City, made some of his most celebrated masterpieces in collaboration with the great structural engineer Felix Candela, in such distant places as Monterrey, Mexico City, and Madrid.

Since then, Monterrey has been, increasingly, inviting world class architects to build in our city, with houses and buildings by Luis Barragán, Ricardo Legorreta, Nicholas Grimshaw, and more recently Tadao Ando, Cesar Pelli, and Norman Foster.

This new global vision of architecture began, in my opinion, about 20 years ago, with the opening of MARCO, Monterrey´s Museum of Contemporary Art, a beautiful building by Ricardo Legorreta. Since the museum has brought in some of the best architecture exhibitions from around the world, our community has suddenly become increasingly interested in the latest trends of contemporary architecture.

Thanks to this small "cultural revolution," which took place in the city during the early nineties, and to the fact that the younger generations had been increasingly exposed to the whole world either by traveling or by the globalized media, a new generation of clients was born, a generation that was tired of sterile historicisms and of simple and meaningless design, which was presented as "modern" architecture.

Since then, Monterrey, a city with a powerful natural landscape due to the beauty of its huge surrounding mountains, has become fertile land for local architects of all generations. They usually have as their clients a group of well-educated and extensively traveled people who have very high expectations for their architectural commissions.

Today, after more than a century devoted to hard work and industrial production, and with a city going through a process of intense densification and growth, it is the time for Monterrey to find its way into the history of contemporary Mexican architecture—and why not of contemporary world architecture as well, just as Mexico City, Guadalajara, and other smaller Mexican cities have been doing in the last decades.

Pedro Castellanos Lambley, Architect,
Casa Quinces—1930,
Guadalajara, Jalisco

Pedro Castellanos Lambley,
Architect, Casa Quinces—1930,
Guadalajara, Jalisco

Luis Barragán, Architect,
Casa Franco—1929,
Guadalajara, Jalisco

The act of creating architecture is loaded with responsibility. Each creation needs to resolve spatial problems to create places where a person may live well, act freely, and be happy. The goal of Adan Lozano Arquitectos is to evolve the design to meet changing situations, offering coherent architectural answers that are responsive to the reality in which people live.

They are committed to a power close to minimalism that tends to stay with essentials—purity, devoid of too much decoration, and free of geometric shapes and elements. They seek clean and bright spaces that invite relaxation and rest.

Adan Lozano Arquitectos

The principles that govern their work are:

- Respect all of nature
- Design according to the topography of the site
- Maximize the natural light
- Take advantage of the prevailing winds
- Minimize the use of available resources such as water and energy

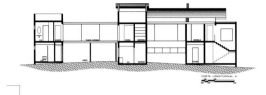

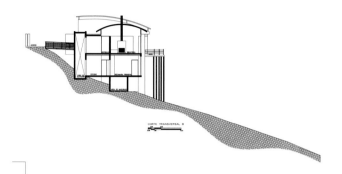

Casa Olinala - 2009
Monterrey, Nuevo Leon

It is always exciting to develop a project in the mountains, with a forest full of oaks, near the city, with fantastic views. The particular topography of this site and the position of the trees were crucial to the project. They were addressed in two modules on two levels, separated and connected by a floating, fully glazed bridge. The rooms are in one module while complementary areas and services are in the other. Coming from the street, the access is by another small, metal bridge with a wooden floor. At this level, the social area is very open, including the dining room, the kitchen, the library, and a small guest bathroom. Two bedrooms with bathroom areas and locker room are on the lower level. Large windows take full advantage of the light and the views of the city, mountain, and forest. Vaulted ceilings with concrete slabs lightened to allow variable inside heights. The place was built with large outside terrace structure with a metal and wood floor that acts as a connector between the two modules and allows the passage of the natural terrain below. An enclosure of opaque glass recessed in the floor separates the area from the dining room off the kitchen area, an element that gives a certain modernity—and ambiguity—to the space. Sobriety and achieved clarity, helped with the selection of a minimum of materials (concrete, metal and glass), the choice of a single color, white, is extended to all the walls, the doors of the rooms, and in some pieces of furniture designed especially for this project. Total transparency in a scene of light and quiet, with a contemporary language in respectful dialogue with nature. The house is a project respecting the environment and conceived as an intervention on the site, talking with nature, which remains present in that place.

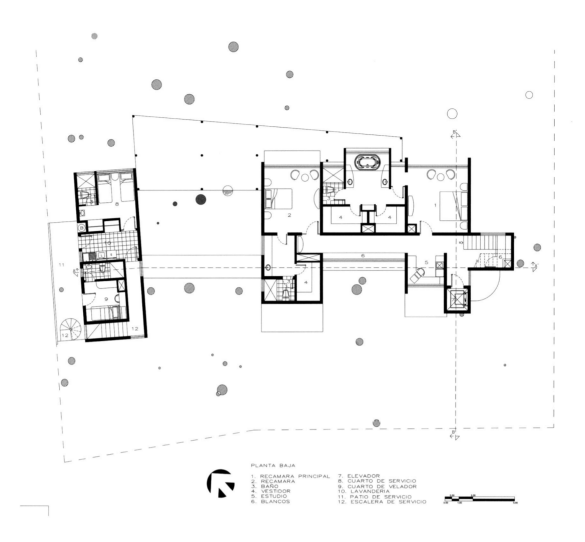

PLANTA BAJA

1. RECAMARA PRINCIPAL
2. RECAMARA
3. BAÑO
4. VESTIDOR
5. ESTUDIO
6. BLANCOS
7. ELEVADOR
8. CUARTO DE SERVICIO
9. CUARTO DE VELADOR
10. LAVANDERIA
11. PATIO DE SERVICIO
12. ESCALERA DE SERVICIO

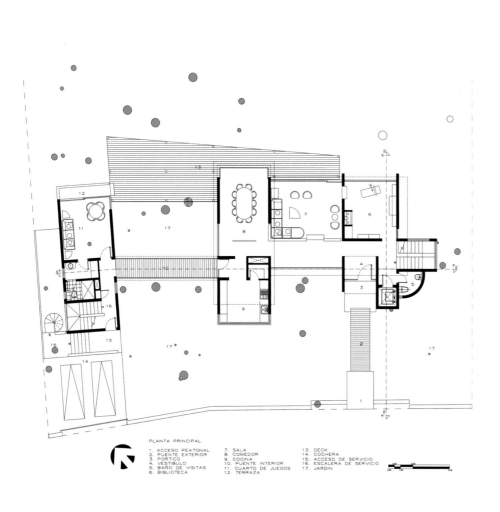

PLANTA PRINCIPAL

1. ACCESO PEATONAL
2. PUENTE EXTERIOR
3. PORTICO
4. VESTIBULO
5. BAÑO DE VISITAS
6. BIBLIOTECA
7. SALA
8. COMEDOR
9. COCINA
10. PUENTE INTERIOR
11. CUARTO DE JUEGOS
12. TERRAZA
13. DECK
14. COCHERA
15. ACCESO DE SERVICIO
16. ESCALERA DE SERVICIO
17. JARDIN

Agraz Arquitectos' path is marked by a constant and deliberate effort toward synthesis and purification. This is instrumental to principal Ricardo Agraz's craft and is the result of his dedication to the work and learning through experience. For Agraz Arquitectos, only by working closely with the client / user is viable architecture possible in terms of identification and durability.

Their inspirations and discoveries come from reflections on aesthetic experiences and memories, in line with Luis Barragán, confident that art is "staged remembrance."

Agraz Arquitectos

At the same time, and occupying all their work, there is a constant yearning to find the stimuli needed to feed aesthetic inquiries in contemporary art. It has long been a clear concern to find a voice with which to express and share their obsessions: beauty, the user, careful design, sensuality, the climate, and modernity. This voice is the thread of the work at Agraz Arquitectos and every day it gains more confidence, meaning, and musicality.

SECTION A-A'

0 1 2 3 4 5

24 HG HOUSE - 2009
Zapopan, Jalisco

HG house is designed for a family where the masculine presence overwhelms any other. This is the idea from which the house's design comes. In addition to the firm's tradition, cars are placed beneath the dwelling by a half level ramp. Garage and service areas are set there, while the house goes up another half level to the main entrance, where a reception lobby and a small bathroom are located.

Next comes one of the most interesting spots in the house: the terrace, dining, living, and family room in a single spatial display without divisions. On one side is the kitchen, separated from the previously described unit by a ramp stairway coming up from the basement. Therefore, entering the house by the garage reaches the same point as entering by the main door. One ends up in the upper level within the same quality features of the mahogany and glass structure.

A generously dimensioned studio for the four boys is set in the second floor, providing them independence from all social activity that might take place in the lower level areas. And right next to this studio are a couple of bedrooms for two boys each, with their very own bath and dressing rooms, leading to a terrace that was conceived as the meeting area for brothers.

The privileged location in the project is the master bedroom, divided into a shared bathroom area with separate dressing rooms that ultimately come together in a light-generating patio, which enjoys the treetop view.

Volumetrically the house is a series of structures that create a harmonious play of shadows throughout the day.

The House is grounded in an intermediate level and is anchored by a central plate that carries the great cube covering this volume lengthways. As this structure comes out in the second level, it becomes a protected shutter belvedere, making the main bedroom an outside observatory.

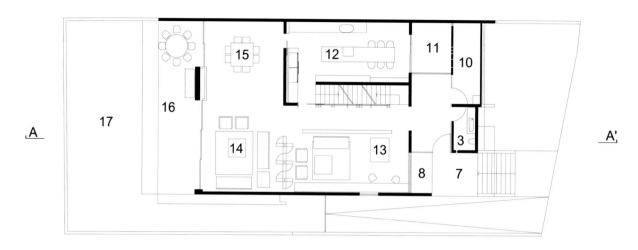

GROUND FLOOR

0 1 2 3 4 5

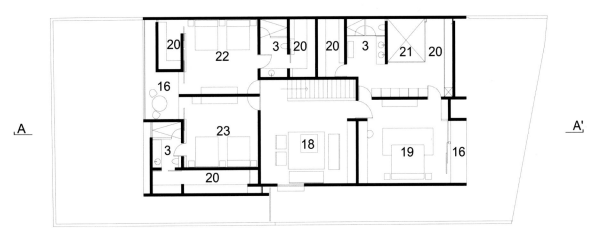

A

A'

FIRST FLOOR
0 1 2 3 4 5

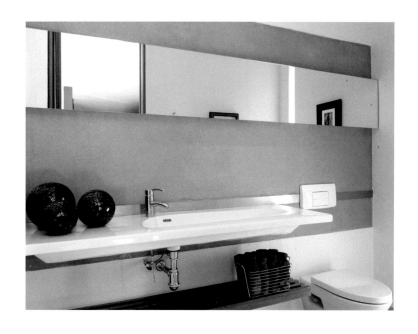

Alejandro Herrasti Arquitectos seeks the creation of space, mature essence, individuality, and a strong, individual personality. Composition, equilibrium, integration, form, texture, color, and proportions are words that some people have associated with their work. Noteworthy within the context of contemporary architecture is the restoration of old artisan techniques, such as wood floors treated with bees wax, exotic wood, and bone inlays in wood paneling and doors, exquisite floor designs in marble and wood, Venetian stucco, and the use of handcrafted leather and shagreen skin.

Alejandro Herrasti Arquitectos

"The sober architectural design
serves as the framework
for an elegant interior environment
whose character is determined
by its city enclave."

Salon: Project A

Dining room: Project B

Dining room: Project A

Salon: Project C

Vestibule: Project A

38   Half bath/powder room: Project B

Library: Project B

Salon: Project A

Salon: Project B

Salon: Project B

Salon: Project B

Architect Jacobo Micha Mizrahi, studied architecture at Universidad Anahuac and is dedicated to architectural design. He has developed hotel, commercial, and residential architecture, including residential and interior design. In 1992, he founded Archetonic, a company dedicated to the architectural design, construction, management, and promotion of works in Mexico.

Archetonic, S.A. de C.V.

Hotel Los Cabos - 2003
Cabo Real, Baja California Sur

Located in the tourist corridor of Cabo Real in Baja California Sur, from the road you can see the façade and the arch, a symbol which has come to represent Hotel Los Cabos. From the lobby you can see the Sea of Cortez, the desert, and the starting point towards different areas of the hotel.

Contemporary architecture based on large walls, gardens, and internal corridors that are integrated into the desert environment provide physical and spiritual rest spaces.

The hotel can be accessed by the motor lobby consisting of a circular water element lined by two rows of palm trees that, in turn, mark the arch of the façade. In the lobby, you can see the mirror of water that integrates with the horizon of the sea and of the fall of a curtain of water 20 meters tall.

At the lobby level are suites with terraces and private pools, all of them with sea views. The hotel has 204 junior suites with terraces and views to the sea, plus thirty-eight casitas, each with a pool on its roof top.

On the lower level, you can find Bar El Suspiro overlooking the curtain of water and the sea, banqueting rooms with a capacity for 800 people, the business center equipped with all services and equipped with leading-edge technology, plus the spa and gym. Outdoor areas at the beach level are integrated into the central part with a swimming pool. There are two large infinity swimming pools that integrate with the sea.

Arquitectos Interiores was founded in 2005 by Maruicio Ramiriz Pizarro, FCIDI, an interior designer from the Art Institute of Fort Lauderdale, and architect Guadalupe Avila Mendez, FCIDI, who holds a Master's degree in architecture from the Universidad Autonoma de Yucatan.

The firm's work has been published in several books and magazines and is recognized by authorities in architecture and design worldwide, from space planning to a finishing materials selection.

Arquitectos Interiores

Arquitectos Interiores is committed to enhance the quality of inhabitable spaces by the means of a better and more complete interior design service.

Rubik Restaurant—2010
Merida, Yucatan

Located on the upper level of a shopping plaza, Rubik was conceived as a youth-oriented but elegant eating place. The design criteria was to develop an experience that built upon Merida's new wave of high quality gourmet restaurants. The space is outfitted with dark painted walls, carpet, and porcelain floors with aluminum compound elements. The project maximized the environment by using the full width of the area and placing the bar as a focal point at the end corner, concealing the service corridor and pulling the view to the back of the restaurant. Muted shades of white and orange are used to color the dining area, while the bar is a bit brighter in tone. The featured metal bar serves as an oasis to its thirsty customers. Cocktail tables behind the bar seating stand on dark, single legs. Chairs, however, are on colored, patterned upholstery. Diners can enjoy subtly different venues on every visit. The most popular seats in the place are those in the front, a terrazzo-like area where you can drink or dine, either in a booth, table, or standing alone with an unobstructed view to the city.

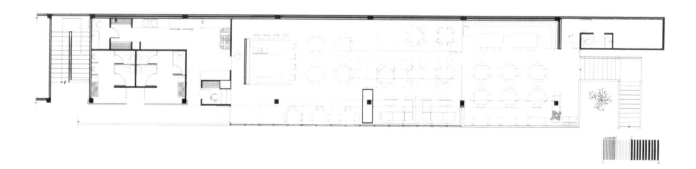

ARCO Arquitectura Contemporánea is an innovative company specializing in property development and interior architecture. The company's experience in Mexico and abroad is evident in the superior quality, transparency, and continuous personal service. The company considers that true architecture is developed based on customer satisfaction, by the use of a language that shapes and expresses the intention in an aesthetic and functional result.

ARCO Arquitectura Contemporánea

ARCO projects are the result of combining forms, colors, and textures that go beyond fulfilling a function. The spaces have a unique language in which materials are more than just structure—they become expressive elements. By adding the spatial experience, aesthetic value, and satisfaction of the client's needs, they transform the construction into an architectonic result.

ARCO Arquitectura Contemporánea was founded by architects Bernardo Lew and José Lew and has more than fifteen years of professional experience in Mexico and the US.

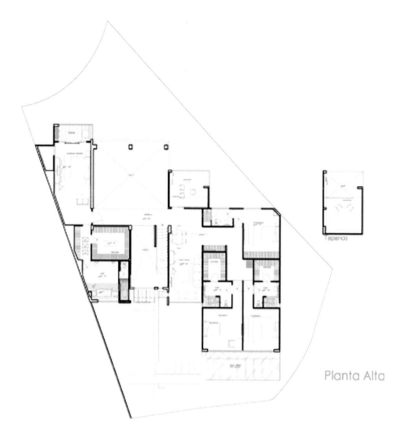

Planta Alta

Casa LC—2011
Mexico DF

This house is located inside of a very exclusive residential development in Mexico City.
It is situated in one of the areas with more economic growth in the last years, but the design
preserves the needed privacy, security, and tranquility for the residents. The site of the house is
surrounded by fantastic landscape that includes an excellent golf course.

The remodeling project for this house was a big challenge that combined the integration of
the indoors and outdoors with important alterations for a warm and contemporary ambiance.
There was also a modification to add a needed bedroom. The original design had great windows
that were left to take advantage of the views and natural light.

Some changes to the main façade were made to give more privacy. Some elements were
added to restrict access inside the premises. The garage was modified. Two columns made of
archeological stone were also incorporated to create a geometric composition in front of the large
windows. The main access has a corridor with a water mirror that runs towards the house and
communicates vertically. The combination of elements and materials on the exterior resulted in
the new image the house required and is a perfect balance between harmony, sensibility, and
warmth.

The interior has generous, two-story spaces, which, combined with the grand windows
in both façades, give excellent natural light and views. The staircase leads to a bridge that
separates the public and private areas. Towards one end of the bridge, the master bedroom is
located and, towards the other, the rest of the bedrooms and a family room are found.

Planta Baja

0 1 2 3   5 MTS   10 MTS
ESCALA GRAFICA

The rapid technological development that has ruled the last decades is reflected in the creative process, leading to the strengthening of multidisciplinary work. Founded with the clear intention to investigate and develop new techniques for architecture in the contemporary city, AT 103 has developed a multidisciplinary team. They share the needs for both an integration of logistics capabilities and a multiplicity of knowledge. Each member of the team contributes his or her particular field of expertise. They share a commitment to innovation. Their methodology seeks to identify their specialty's specific modes of action, taking multimedia technology as a tool for understanding the TIME and SPACE.

AT 103

The building types are constantly changing. Through the use of computer technology and simple handicraft, AT 103 achieves what they call "low tech–high resolution" effects. The skin becomes a garment that protects the body while the body contains all program activities. The main point lies in the relationship between various spaces, and their ability to change over time, rather than the spaces themselves.

Casa Romero—2006
Querétaro, Querétaro

The project responded to the specific needs of a four-member family. The design developed out of an existing foundation, from which it was necessary to define clarity on the volumes that constitute the house, considering the use of materials and the program that each box contains.

The stone box is the hermetic one; it contains the principal bathroom and services areas, such as storage, housekeeper's room, and garage. The wooden box contains all public areas: living room, dining room, studio, bar, kitchen, TV room, plus guests' and kids' rooms. Access is through the void generated in between these two, connecting directly to the living room, a two-storied space where the main stairs and the linking bridge between the boxes are located.

A metallic structure was proposed to fulfill the need for fast construction and lightness over the existing foundation. Prefabricated materials were used and, based on its modulation, they were then perforated to generate the visual relation in-between interior and exterior.

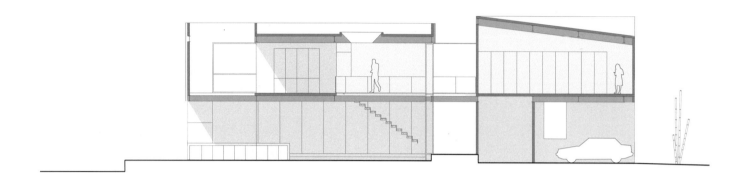

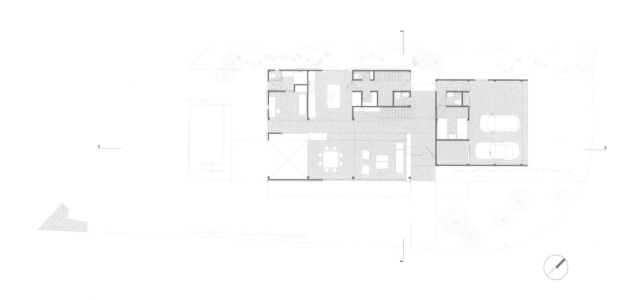

A person reacts to an architectural space. If the space is sensitive, in composition and harmony, the person will reflect what is perceived.

Bulnes 103 Grupo de Diseño's philosophy is that they can only design for a person when they have tried to come to know him/her completely—both essence and spirit, past, present, and a projection into the future, searching through their human, emotional, spiritual, and literal language. The result is to, maybe, make the architecture express the clients.

This was an aspiration of Greeks, Egyptians, Mayans, and other great cultures. Their architecture was the most powerful artistic expression, the most vigorous of humanity in its time.

Bulnes 103 Grupo de Diseño

The firm believes that an architect has the great responsibility to create, in composition, harmony, and beauty, all his works in accordance to the environment and the time.

Pure creativity by itself does not exist. Research, common sense, and logic, in the firm's exhaustive analysis, lead to the originality of the resulting design. The architectural process is much more than the planning of function or shape. It is the art of giving function to the shape ... and shape to the function at the same time .

Casa de la Cañada—2009
Monterrey, Nuevo Leon

This house is located on the old road to the hacienda San Agustin. The site is heavily forested with a stream running through it. This work of Mother Nature produces a great visual and emotional backdrop for the life of the house and its owners.

The house is on three large levels, supported by a tower of 41 meters, and two levels with heights of 24 meters. This tower provides support through tensors that are located on level two and level three, strategically and structurally completed with two top tensioners. This has resulted in a set of volumes in cantilever, all of them supported by the central tower, which includes an elevator through five levels and a set of stairs.

This design is due, not only in the structural sense, to the necessity of creating supports that avoided damaging any trees on the site and protecting the site from the water runoff, all the while respecting the natural channel of the river.

First level: At the height of the trunk and crown of the trees is the main hall, the stairs with additional access to the upper levels, to the main lift, garages, and services, at this point connecting with a bridge of six meters wide by thirty-six meters.

Second level: In the middle, or between the cup of the trees, the social area is located with three terraces favoring views toward the foliage and the waterfall. Coming through is the (glass step) gallery, which offers a spectacular view of the lush vegetation surrounding it.

Third level: Private area including three bedrooms, with their dressing room and bathrooms, as well as a broad family area, with its terrace and panoramic view. The other two bedrooms have their own terrace. The roof level contains a reception area and an office.

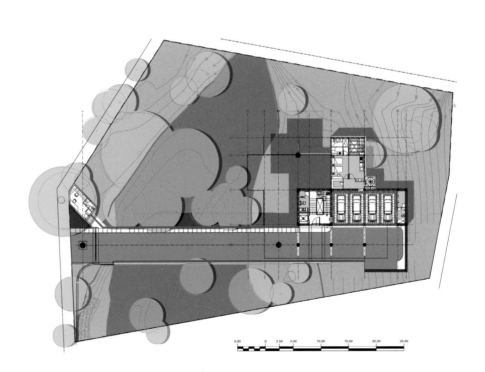

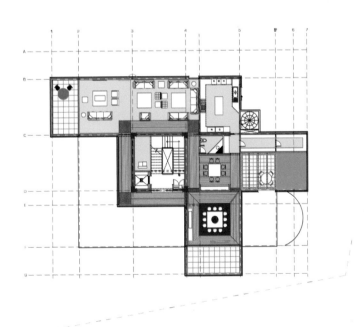

For Elias Rizo Arquitectos, everything is summed up in one simple idea: create beautiful spaces that improve their client's everyday life. It's about fulfilling the client's needs, with a commitment to honesty, service, and quality. Architecture not only gives people eternity and shelter, but it embraces them; it is a contained space that holds the course of their lives. It is always there to teach them, but, above all, it gives them fantasies.

Elias Rizo Arquitectos

Elias Rizo Arquitectos believes they are a driving force for their culture and context, having an unavoidable impact on their project's surroundings, which entails great responsibility. Therefore, it is essential to understand, learn, and create despite the risks. Nothing can be gained without risk. They are committed with those who inhabit space, willing to experience both the good and bad that architecture represents. The firm is confident that through architecture, one can transform fantasy into reality.

Ground Floor
1.- Entry 2.- Lobby 3.- Garage
4.- Storage 5.- Service patio 6.- Service room
7.- Laundry 8.- Wc 9.- Kitchen 10.- Dining room
11.- Living room 12.- Terrace 13.- Garden 14.- Pool
15.- Wc 16.- Machine room

First Floor
17.- Master bedroom 18.- Studio 19.- Gym
20.- Bedroom 1 21.- Bedroom 2 22.- Bookshelf
23.- Wardrobe 24.- Wc 25.- Balcony

Casa RO—2010
Guadalajara, Jalisco

The site is located in a well established residential area. The existing house, built in the 1960s, with its straight lines, honest circulation, communication with the exterior, and usage of materials, represented the architecture of its time. All these hints help the architect decipher the project and set in motion the arduous work of intervention while respecting its essence.

The project consisted of the restoration of the old house, which was really deteriorated. The house had several failed previous remodels, but there was a lot to rescue. It began with the demolition of some of the adjacent areas. It was all about precise work, demanded by these particular clients—a young family with a desire for quality aesthetics—using a scalpel to cut away the outdated and excessive from the essence of the building. One of the main goals was to create a warm space distanced from current architectural stereotypes and trends. The materials used became the main protagonists for the space: wood as the prevailing material in façades and interiors, and stone, which was selected to complement with what was already in place. The restoration keeps almost all the original marble flooring on the ground floor.

The house revolves around two main spaces, the two-storied foyer and the terrace. The foyer is restored and destined to become a sculptural area. The gnarled tree stumps that the visitor finds in the foyer offer a stark contrast to the clean lines and precise disposition of the wood furnishings that cover the walls. The new terrace is where the family interacts and spends most of the day. It is open to the garden and aims to take advantage of the temperate weather, allowing for year-round use.

The site's orientation defines the design of the façades, with a translucent skin that solves the issue of solar radiation for the bedrooms, acquiring a duality between an open space and an isolated one. A large part of the wooden "brise soleil" in the back façade is mounted on rails so it can open up to allow more light to enter, while also allowing for varying configuration of the façade. The defining characteristic of this restoration project is the precision of the design and construction.

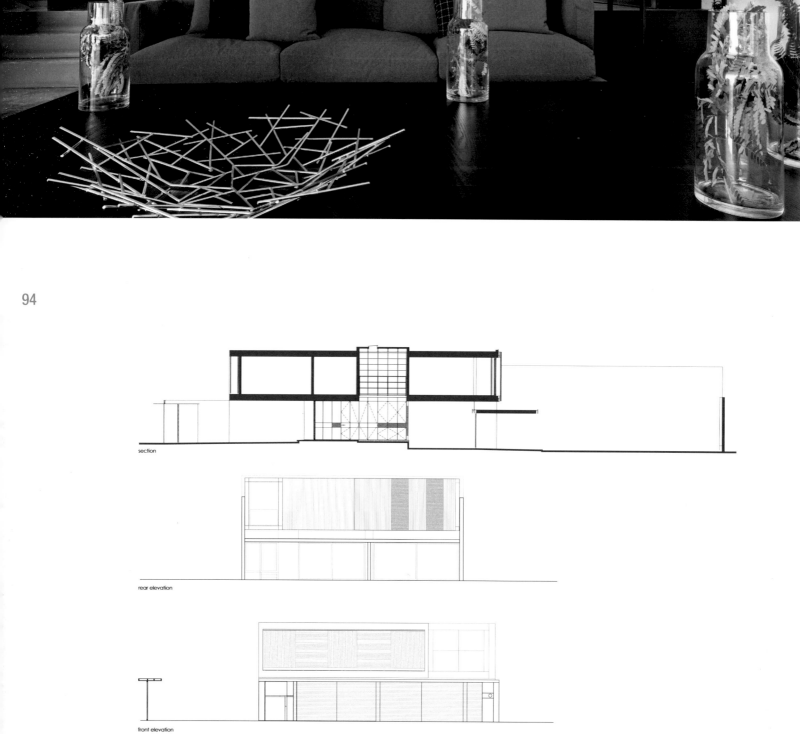

section

rear elevation

front elevation

FRENTEarquitectura is a Mexican architectural practice formed by young professionals whose main goal is to create innovative and "responsible" architecture. In this case, responsible is meant to be the "ability to respond" (to give a clever answer to a specific need).

FRENTEarquitectura

They prioritize the analysis of the specific circumstances of each project (place, people, and time) over the creative activity, thus to be able to establish the real needs to be fulfilled.

In FRENTE, they generate simple architecture, of clear shapes and strong concepts, giving each project its own character.

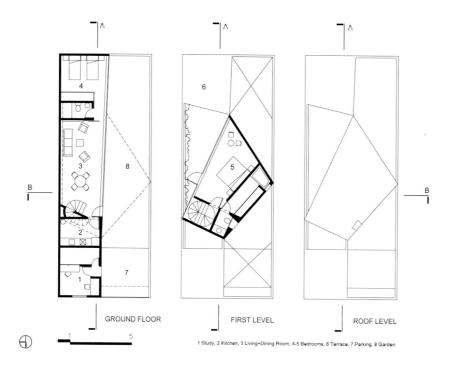

GROUND FLOOR   FIRST LEVEL   ROOF LEVEL

1 Study, 2 Kitchen, 3 Living+Dining Room, 4-5 Bedrooms, 6 Terrace, 7 Parking, 8 Garden

**Mixcoac House—2006
Mexico DF**

The project consists of demolishing an old house and building a new one with a very tight budget, preserving only the street-front façade.

Because of the chaotic context of the lot, the main idea was to turn the house inward to a widespread space. To achieve this, the ground floor was divided lengthwise, placing the construction on the left side, taking the fullest possible advantage of the depth of the lot for the garden.

Special care was given to scale and perspective, trapezoidal shapes, and varying the window modulation to obtain visual effects that underline the initial idea emphasizing vanishing points.

In addition, a cloudy sky printed on canvas was placed at the rear wall to hide the neighboring building and to dramatize the impression of spaciousness on the small lot.

The house has a living and dining room, bedroom, study, kitchen, and bathroom on the ground floor. The master bedroom with its closet, bathroom, and terrace, is on the upper level.

SECTION A   SECTION B

Using a sober, contemporary language supported by the warmth of different natural materials, architect Gilberto L. Rodríguez's spaces acquire a timeless quality free of trends. Says the architect, "In my architecture, I seek a neutral framework that can coexist equally well with a minimalist interior design as with an eclectic concept with elements from diverse eras and origins."

GLR Arquitectos

Rodrigez holds a degree from the Tecnológico de Monterrey and a Master's of Architecture from Harvard University. As the architect in charge of the architecture and interior design, he has developed a wide portfolio that includes residential projects as well as important mixed-use developments.

GLR Arquitectos are currently working on projects in several cities in Mexico, the United States, and Saudi Arabia.

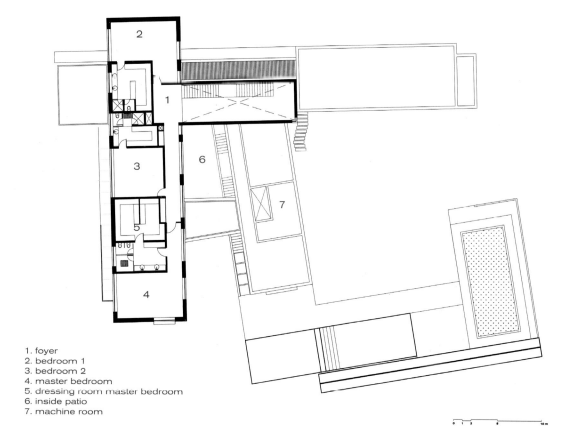

1. foyer
2. bedroom 1
3. bedroom 2
4. master bedroom
5. dressing room master bedroom
6. inside patio
7. machine room

CASA BC—2010
Monterrey, Nuevo Leon

This project is in a privileged topographic situation, situated above its surrounding neighbors. This allows the house to enjoy excellent vistas towards the national park of Chipinque in the south, as well as towards the east, which is dominated on the horizon by the "Cerro de la Silla," an emblematic hill within the boundaries of the city of Monterrey. The access to the site is located on the north side, ascending through a long slope that leads to the highest level, where the home is located. With simple, pure geometric volumes, but rather challenging structural solutions, the project evokes an image of lightness within a language of heavy and massive volumes.

Although color does not yet have an important presence in the firm's work, this project takes an important step forward into the exploration of new materials, using black granite and the white exposed concrete in addition to the personality that the amount of exposed steel elements gives to the building. Finally, it is important to mention that, beyond its bio-climatic function, the implementation of green roofs is a way to integrate the landscape, trying to conserve the natural surroundings of the zone, always dominated by the presence of the splendid Sierra Madre mountain range.

The house was conceived as a "sustainable house" since the beginning, so it was studied for energetic efficiency, which analyzed the sun's trajectory and the prevailing winds in diverse seasons of the year. As a result of these studies, the house has multiple systems of insulation, like its double walls with an ecological insulator; double windows with low emissivity (Low-E) glass; systems of pluvial water harvesting and gray water treatment for irrigation, solar paddles for pool heating and garden illumination, solar water heaters, hydroponic heating systems to reduce power consumption, south-oriented skylights, as well as a landscape project with native vegetation.

When Hernandez Silva Arquitectos begins any project, objectives and intentions are established, creating a path that guides the development of an idea without any preconceived perceptions, taking as a critical element the analysis of site and user. They consider the user as the center of all decisions they make, creating a strict and exhaustive analysis of physical and spiritual needs resulting in a broad program. They propose spaces as gathering places, where life experiences and human activities develop, emphasizing contemplation and spirituality. The concept is the synthesis of the analysis and its context; it is the driving force that gives the project its identity.

The concept is divided into three parts:

- *The formal concept:* it is the expressive intention they look for in the project.
- *The functional concept:* this is the location proposals, space relations, and the journey between them.
- *The structural project:* the criteria used in the constructive elements and materials to give the physical shape.

Hernandez Silva Arquitectos

They understand the city, rather than a siting of constructions, as the sum of individual and collective efforts to weave history. For them, tradition is neither static nor old, but something that nurtures, modifies, and enriches day-by-day. They see it as a social value to architecture, something that provides within measure into a city's or community's heritage.

They define style as a way of making things and not as preconceived shapes that try to repeat a commercial formal language; in fact, more than looking for an specific style, they work in contents. Light, transparency, and depth—this is the true expressive value of space. They are aware of both materials and financial means. Their raw material is the space—understanding movement and human scale.

Even though the project is delivered by an abstract concept, it must culminate in a project defined by constructible, living elements. They know that the commercial market is important, but they never subordinate architecture to it. It is not about concessions. Architecture must keep a constant dialogue with arts. The contents of architecture are arguments that support the project proposal. Each project is a unique universe of challenge that must be deciphered.

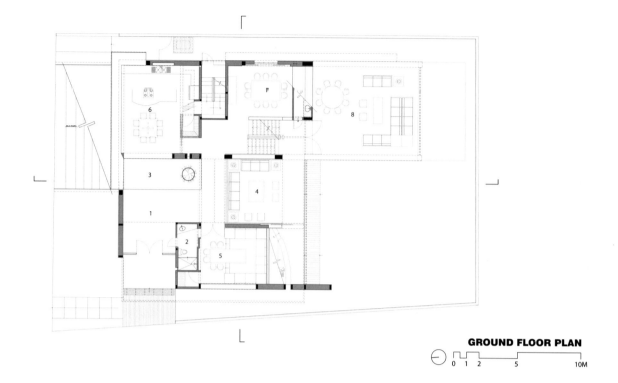

1. MAIN ENTRANCE
2. POWDER ROOM
3. INNER PATIO
4. LIVING ROOM
5. STUDIO
6. KITCHEN
7. DINNING ROOM
8. TERRACE

GROUND FLOOR PLAN

0 1 2   5   10M

Casa Godoy—2009
Zapopan, Jalisco

120

The house is located in a private neighborhood outside the city, where the land is flat and located in a corner, with neighbors to the south and east sides, the west containing a large line of trees that separates the house from the street and takes a turn to the north, where both entrances lie: one pedestrian and another one for cars. There are two floating structures: the structure on the left is a large box covered in gray stone that levitates over the street, opening a gap where the cars are parked. The second structure is transparent and light, larger and higher, which shows the pedestrian entrance. It is a volume of windows to the north and west sheltered by a white steel lattice, which considers the relationship with the sun, as this orientation is extremely harsh in the city.

The transparent volume at the entrances expands by the side of the trees, the lattice covers its front face and is secured to a vertical wall at the back, which eventually blocks the heat from the west. Two walls in the back rise and bend horizontally to create a great flying ceiling of 36 feet over the garden and pool, supporting a second floor where the master bedroom is located so that it gets a complete open view to the garden, which is surrounded by woodlands.

The entrance platform is elevated because the house has a semi-basement; thereby, it is allowed to generate different, uneven levels, opening the flow in several directions. The inside is completely open, with almost all the walls in the same direction. This is quite evident from the courtyard entrance, which is a well-lit, double height gap, where the main circulations converge, one vertical and the other a translucent glass bridge connecting the two ends on the first floor.

The house structure is steel, built during a period when this material was at a low price, allowing the building of an almost floating house. The house opens with a long and folding window system in the background, integrating the garden into the interior, making social spaces in a fully integrated large terrace with a garden and pool. This allows living with the cool Guadalajara's weather. The dining room looks out above the terrace and communicates above the garden with the kitchen and studio. The two stairs set off from the basement to the second floor, one leads to the services and the other weaves the social and private spaces of the house.

The roofs are flat on the front but slightly declined on the back due to construction regulations; they are covered with coated yellow ceramic. The walls are mostly smooth, the floors are marble and wood, and the carpentry is all in dark colors. White steel is used on many elements of the house.

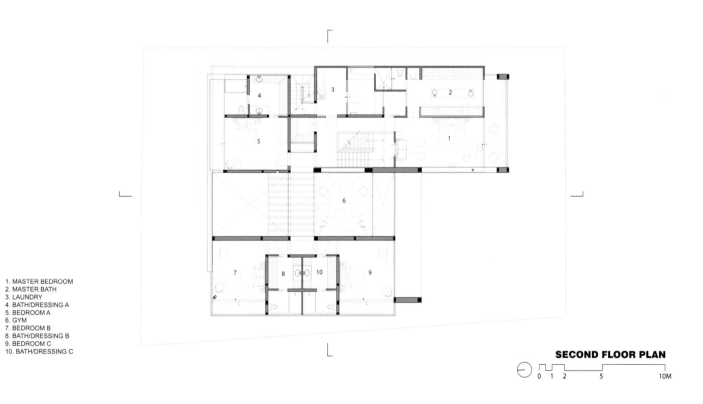

1. MASTER BEDROOM
2. MASTER BATH
3. LAUNDRY
4. BATH/DRESSING A
5. BEDROOM A
6. GYM
7. BEDROOM B
8. BATH/DRESSING B
9. BEDROOM C
10. BATH/DRESSING C

SECOND FLOOR PLAN

0 1 2   5   10M

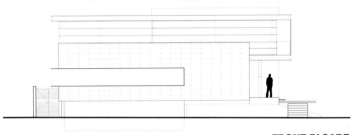

FRONT FACADE

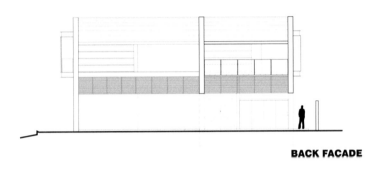

BACK FACADE

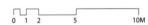

0 1 2   5   10M

Hierve is a small, multi-disciplinary design firm based in Mexico City and London. The firm was established in 1999 by Alejandro Villarreal, with the purpose of serving society through high quality projects in architecture, product design, the visual arts, and the development of business models. At the core of its belief system is the underlying idea that creativity should not serve itself, but should serve society as a whole.

The company is small and it has a global approach. They team up with highly qualified professionals who bring their talent from Mexico City (Mexico), London (UK), Boulder (USA), Sofia (Bulgaria), Munich (Germany), among others. Since the beginning, the company has

Hierve

sought to find a balance between efficiency and artistic thrust, between practicality and creative insight. They believe that a high level of creativity can be achieved alongside a high level of efficiency and business sense.

When developing a project, they open themselves up to the past, to history. They believe there is a great amount of information in past achievements and efforts. However, they are also open to innovation, to new insights and ideas that can bring up something good and useful. At the same time, they believe that each project should be unique; each project should emerge from its own specific conditions and requirements. They take the time to listen, to research, and to understand.

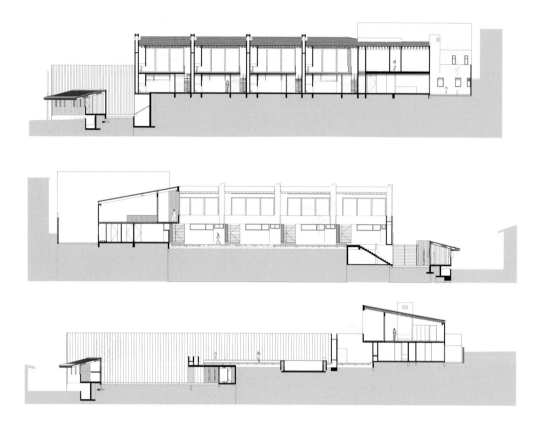

Santa Maria—2010
Valle de Bravo, Mexico

Santa Maria is a housing development located in a historic, protected site in the heart of Valle de Bravo, a small colonial city dating from 1530, which is two hours away from Mexico City. This historic town has a strong physical context and is found on the outskirts of a man-made lake. The site is located a hundred yards from the church of Santa Maria Ahuacatlan, a colonial church that dates back to the sixteenth century. The project was conceived as a weekend retreat from Mexico City's busy lifestyle and it includes nine townhouses and some amenities that provide an almost hotel-like experience.

From the very early stages of design, a strong connection with the site was sought by responding to its topography, to the existing vegetation, to the views of the lake, to the neighboring buildings, to the width of the streets, etc. Also, they tried to make a more conceptual connection by incorporating the flavor of the rich natural and rural landscape surrounding Valle de Bravo. That's why they decided to incorporate long trenches along the project and fill them with natural river stones and vegetation.

The spirit and aspirations of the place were sought out, trying to bring them to their next stage of evolution, where the new structure respectfully talks about the past, is firmly rooted in the present, and gives a sense of direction for the future. Maybe that's why this project constantly tries to be physically anchored to the ground and at the same time tries to float and fly away in the sky.

JC Name Arquitectos SC takes a disciplinary approach to its vast array of projects. This design and architecture firm takes on the risk for crafting a unique composition of forms, colors, and materials, creating a special language for a constantly changing region within a growing economy.

The prevalence of the firm's architecture relies on the use of forms, contents, and concepts. JC Name creates lifestyles, from high end residential houses to small retail stores, and from hotels to offices, and call centers to art spaces.

JC Name Arquitectos SC

The recognition of the firm's projects includes a wide arrangement of narratives that share a common language under the special attention to innovation, detailing, crafting, and technology. With a team of people that ranges in ages, experiences, and world travelers, the office shares a common thought: the search for new lifestyles and the passion for innovative design and architecture.

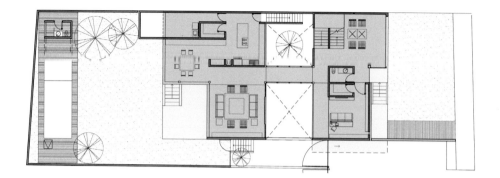

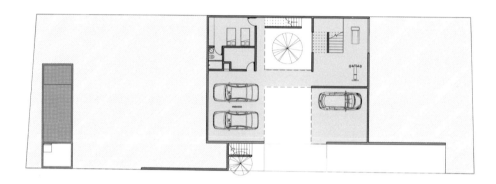

CASA ML—2008
Guadalajara, Jalisco

During ML's design process for the house, questions and resolutions arose in which there was a constant search for volumetric experimentation. The concept is based on a central distribution through a patio interrupted by a bridge. This generalization of the patio constitutes memories from the past and the Latin-American colonial house prototype, perhaps a vernacular and regional thought, but with deep investigation on aesthetics and experimental forms in relation to program and design.

The floor plan, interrupted by a patio, generates two diaphanous prisms conceptually united by a ribbon that goes all through the house, from the front to the back. It is about a formal relation of dislocated forms that generate visual constraints and constructively unfolds in a true dialogue between interior and exterior. The program allows the partition for this volumetric study and the separation of public spaces versus private.

The circulation is always to the center, and it is through these elements that the form is broken. Stairs and windows generate visual and photogenic constructions in all the assembly. The project represents a study in deep perspectives; openness and transparencies, red, gray, and white colors emphasize the aesthetics about the use of alien materials to the residential typology, but that conjugate warmth and quality at the same time.

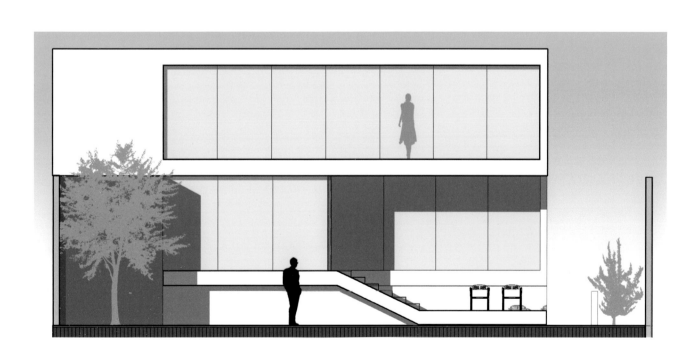

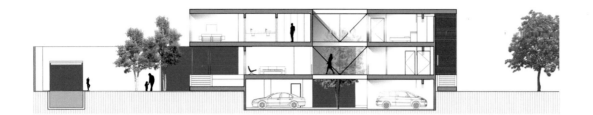

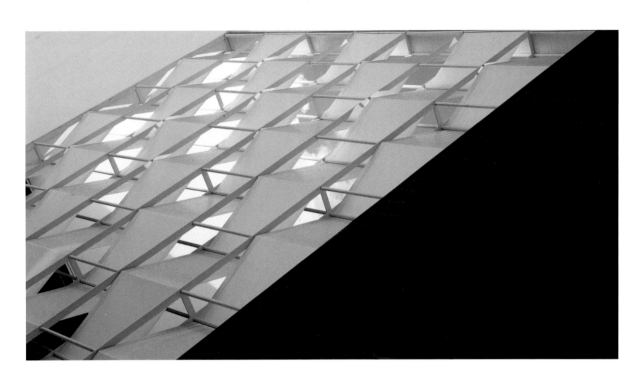

With eleven years of experience in real estate development and architecture, the group Higuera + Sanchez (1996–2007) evolved into JSª Arquitectos.

JSª focuses on design development, strengthening its best known and awarded activities, which are architecture and creation of innovative real estate projects and spaces. JSª establishes alliances with the best construction firms to obtain the highest quality for its projects, concentrating its efforts in accentuating the culture of service for its clients.

JSª Arquitectos

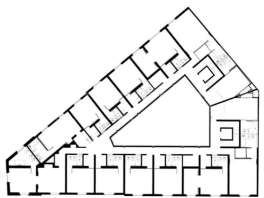

Condesa DF—2005
Mexico DF

This hotel project recycled an apartment building dating from 1928, catalogued by Mexico's National Beaux Arts Institute. The perimeter of the building was preserved up to the first corridor, which was restored to its original state.

The inside of the building was demolished to build an opened patio, which is the central space of the project. A dialogue between architectures goes on in here; the circulations leading to the hotel rooms are turned facing this open, public space, where the building connects to the outside.

Folding aluminum shades open into the patio, transforming the space. The shades virtually extend the corridors and offer a interplay of seeing and not being seen. The sun travels in the patio, generating shadows and giving greater depth to the space.

The patio and the two levels that were added to the original structure were built with a steel structure and reinforced concrete flagstones, so they would blend in with the preexisting quarry and white cement finishes.

Restaurant and bar services are located at the ground level to make the best use for the pedestrian flow at the street level. On the first and second floors, the hotel rooms have a balcony in the original spaces of the building.

On the preexisting roof, an additional level was built for suites with a private terrace. This level is pulled behind the main façade to avoid being seen from the street. Crowning the building is a terrace with a spa and resting areas for the guests. This terrace in the evenings becomes a sushi bar, open for city dwellers.

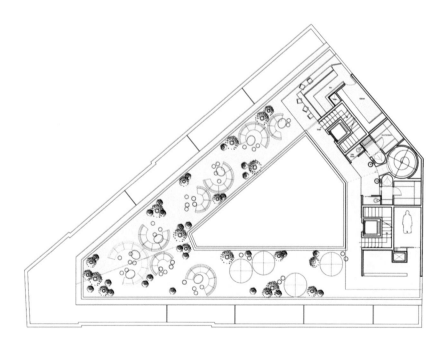

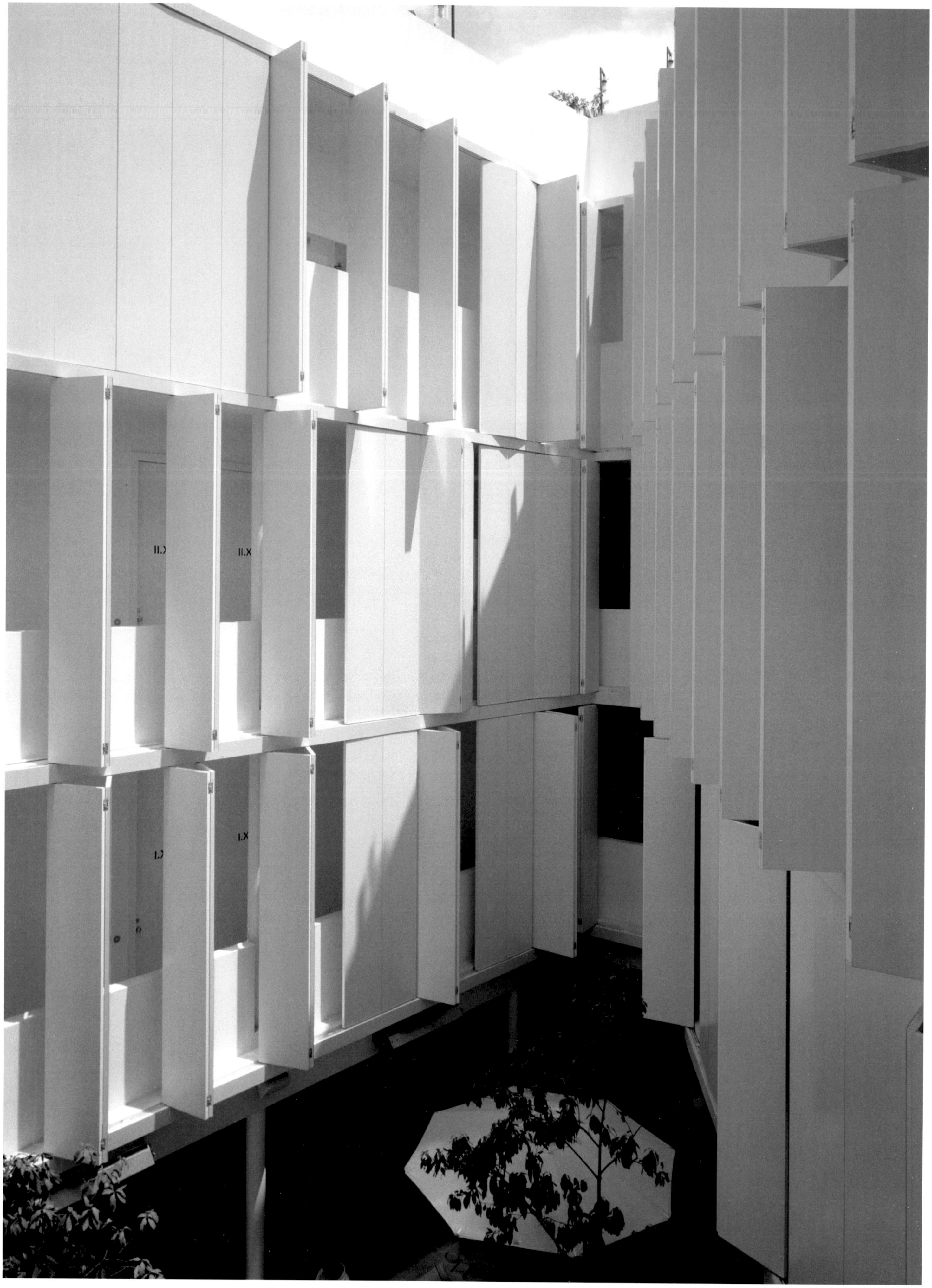
II.X
II.X
I.X
I.X

Elias Kababie graduated from the Faculty of Architecture at Universidad Iberoamericana in Mexico City. He continued his studies at Parsons Design School in New York, specializing in industrial and interior design and complemented those studies with lighting courses at Phillips and architecture courses at Pratt Institute.

His professional career is a balance between architecture, interior design, and product design. His main goal is to achieve perfect synchrony between architecture, interiors, and objects in order to transmit the lifestyle of each one of his clients.

Kababie Arquitectos

Under the motto "back to basics," created projects are proposals beyond creative boundaries with a unique concept that includes technology, current trends, and global expression.

His designs have been published in important magazines and newspapers in Mexico and in other countries and have also received important awards. He has participated in major stores like CAD, Common People, and Casa Palacio. Some of his designs are being sold at the Mexican Gallery of Design and in MUAC and MODO museums in Mexico City.

156   Department Anatole France—2012
Mexico DF

In projects designed by Kababie Arquitectos, it is very important to reflect the client's identity. The architecture and interior design of the space should transform into a mirror of the client's personality, and for this apartment in Polanco, the architect, focused on developing a space designed for the activities and lifestyle of a single man.

The living and dining room areas have a two-storied height and become the center of the project. The large window varies the intensity of the light throughout the day, changing the space according to the time. At night, the area is enhanced by lamps placed strategically throughout the space.

The architect chose a nearly monochromatic palette in which color accents are created by the nature of the materials creating a very harmonious set. There are some details that stand out, such as the great picture on the stairs, the handmade rug, and a bookshelf in the bedroom that was custom-made according to the project's needs. One of the walls was left unfinished to give a high contrast with an industrial touch.

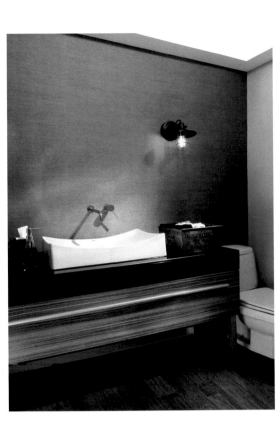

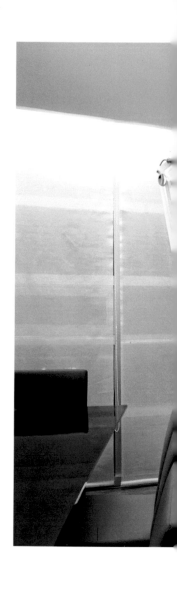

158

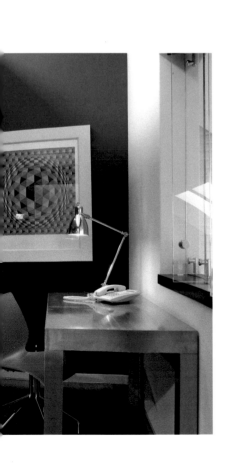

LeAP is a conceptual jump from the linearity of past models of thought to the non-linearity of contemporary complex, critical thinking. They leave behind the sterile, closed, and inflexible formality in favor of the open, unpredictable, and non-deterministic systems that are a reflection of their illusory reality.

LeAP was founded in August of 2001 as an open space to re-think architecture and urbanism. During these years of practice they have had the opportunity to experiment in every scale of architecture, from interior design to urban design.

LeAP Arquitectura

For them, architecture cannot be submitted to fixed rules or conceptions. They believe in experimentation as a way of pushing the boundaries of the discipline, therefore take every project, regardless of the scale, as an opportunity to explore new issues.

CIMA 300
PENTHOUSE

4 recamaras · 4.5 baños   servicios
metros cuadrados en terrazas   60.30
metros cuadrados departamento   376.16
total metros cuadrados   436.46

vista a campo de golf / alberca

CIMA 300—2009
Guadalajara, Jalisco

166

Contemporary trends, innovation in the proposed space, and the current socio-cultural conditions of the city merge into the idea of creating CIMA300, a progressive architectural building expression.

With a timeless approach and sober pallet of materials, the 15-story building creates a harmonic impact on its immediate context. The building is located in the new, high-end residential area of the city, adjacent to Valle Real in the Metropolitan Zone of Guadalajara, Mexico, and is part of the prestigious residential complex of Cima Real.

Its privileged location serves as a platform on which the tower stands. The natural elevation of the land guarantees a splendid view, even in the lowest levels of the building.

The lobby and tower amenities are spaces of unique atmospheres. Each area becomes an environment combining privacy and recreation to captivate the senses of the residents and visitors.

When approaching the building, a sensation of simplicity and elegance reigns through the horizontal expression of its thin terraces that emerge from the main cubic volume in which the main bedrooms are contained. When reaching the double-height main lobby—a breath-taking open space that houses the front desk, a common bar, a multi-purpose room, and a cinema—a sculptural stair emerges and links the lobby to the mezzanine level. The mezzanine houses the gym, interior terrace/bar, spa, and pool.

The building is structured around a series of exposed concrete walls in which the structural loads converge in the heart of the building, where the service module and distributor are located.

Two sets of double-door elevators, one freight elevator, and a service staircase configure the vertical circulation of the building. Recordable pipeline facilities run through the general service area and an independent air conditioning system lies in the interplay of the concrete structural walls.

The architectural plan includes four exclusive apartments per level, each with independent terraces and spectacular views of the city and the adjacent golf course. With an adequate orientation, each apartment consists of three bedrooms and the day area (which includes the kitchen, dining room, and living room) merges into a single space that extends up to the front terrace.

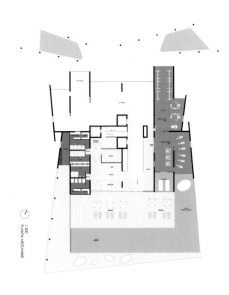

1:200
PLANTA MEZZANINE

1:200
planta lobby

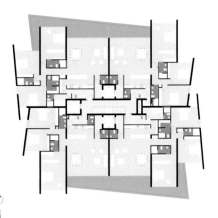

1:150
PLANTA TIPO

In architecture, spaces must communicate with the people who live in them and transmit their lifestyle.

Each project is a commitment to both the interior and exterior that generates a language through all the elements that shape it. The result is an atmosphere that is present in an intimate communication between the architect and his client.

Lopez Duplan Arquitectos

Architect Claudia Lopez Duplan has more than 20 years of experience in the development of residential, corporate, and commercial projects. Her unique sensitivity and style have positioned her in the interior design scene; she has also specialized in residential renovation that gives the spaces a new identity.

In her projects, lighting plays an important role and the use of indirect light, combined with variation of intensity, creates different atmospheres required for each space. Keeping the original architecture is one of the challenges faced in each project, besides the integration of all elements giving that result in a whole new image.

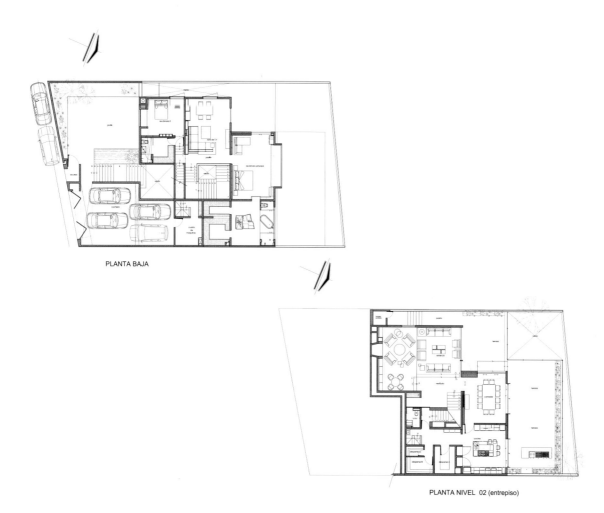

PLANTA BAJA

PLANTA NIVEL 02 (entrepiso)

Casa Lomas Altas—2011
Mexico DF

The original house was built in the early 1980s and is located west of Mexico City. This was a total remodel of both space and image. In addition to interior and exterior renovation, major changes were also made in all the facilities, especially for the unification of the public areas.

The house is divided into three-and-a-half levels. In the intermediate floor, the number and proportion of windows was increased to take advantage of views to the forest and the entrance of natural light. There was also a total change of the window screens to integrate the terraces and open areas to the interior of each space, maintaining a bond with all the services.

All the spaces were unified, using a limited selection of materials. In the interior, wood floors and light marble were combined, and for the kitchen granite was used in the same shade. In the exterior, all the floors and part of the wall are covered with dark gray stone.

In the interior design, the stair is the central axis giving access to the public and private areas of the house. All the walls around it were removed to integrate all the spaces. In the living room, the generous existing height was used to play with the platforms and the indirect lighting, enhancing the deep sensation of the space and highlighting the artwork.

The private areas are located at the top floor, in which large windows were also incorporated to make the most of the views. In the master bedroom, a bookcase designed specifically for the needs of the space that enhances the view and makes it cozier frames the window. The bathroom is a large space from which you can also enjoy spectacular views.

Significant changes were made on all the façades, from structural changes to the incorporation of new finishes for the renewal to be perceived from the entrance. In the gardens surrounding the house, a complete transformation project was also done, respecting an existing large tree that sets the tone for the new image.

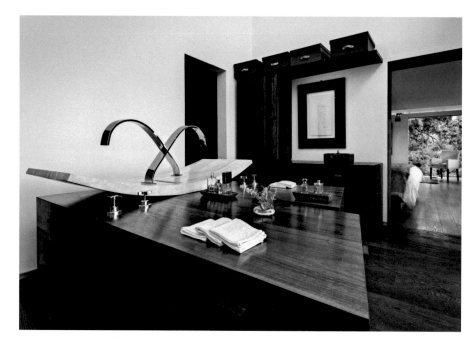

The identity that supports the projects developed by the firm, with headquarters in Mexico City since 1979, comes as a result of the fact that there is not an ulterior ideology forming the language or the materials used. The team works to form unique discourses ascribed to any project.

For Pascal Arquitectos, each practice, each creation is the outcome of particular and determining factors, such as available resources, social, or location context. Everything is exhaustively analyzed. The commitment is at the same time to the client and the final user, as well to the environment and the city. And everything is based upon a unique research process and experimentation using new materials and technologies.

Pascal Arquitectos

The atelier is comprised of a polyfunctional group whose development does not depend on a typology of specialization, which can restrain creativity and innovation. For this reason all kinds of projects are produced at Pascal: residential, corporate, contract, and hospitality, temples or ritual spaces, where—depending on each particular case—besides developing the architecture, the interior, and furniture design, lighting, and landscape are designed as well.

Their work of the last thirty years has built a wealth of knowledge and experience. Among the more representative examples of their work is the Sheraton "Centro Historico" Hotel, located in front of the Alemeda Central and Mediation House in Bosques de las Lomas, which has received worldwide recognition and numerous awards. The firm has also ventured into restoration and recycling projects, cataloged as historical and artistic buildings. One example is the Oriental Bolivia Building, designed in 1962 by architect José Villagrán Garcia. The atelier's work has been widely published.

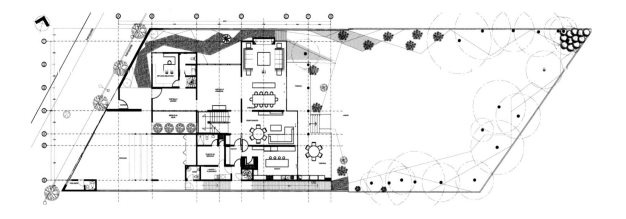

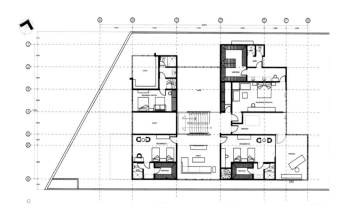

184 Secreto House—2011
Mexico DF

This house was built on two levels, on grounds that include a free area occupied by the garage, a courtyard with reflecting pool, and the garden.

Ground Floor: covered entrance hall, inner hall, two-storied height library, and interior patio, two guest bathrooms, living room with fireplace, dining room, breakfast area, and kitchen with pantry and utility room. Includes room-covered terraces, breakfast area, kitchen, and a barbecue pit.

Upper level: lobby, TV room, master bedroom with bathroom and dressing room, gym, two secondary bedrooms with bathroom and dressing room each, and an outdoor terrace garden. A guest bedroom with bathroom is separated from the rest of the bedrooms, also on this level.

The basic structure is concrete with rebar, concrete walls, red brick, and structural steel elements.

The exterior wall finishes and some interior ones are Galarza stone. Plaster and paint were used for the ceiling and marble was used in the bathrooms. Wet areas are cast with vinyl and enamel paints.

Chiseled exterior concrete floors and marble in various sizes were employed, as designed river boulders were dropped into the water body and the side garden walkway. Walnut flooring and carpet were used in the dressing rooms. Windows were in anodized aluminum with clear glass. There are iron railings and gates, and the garage doors and access were in iron and wood.

Fixed furniture in the library, a two-storied height ceiling lamp, toilets, closets, dressers and cupboards, and doors and baseboards are all made of walnut.

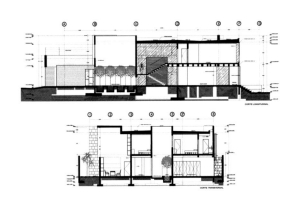

One of the most complex and problematic issues facing humans in this century is building habitat in harmony with nature. At Picciotto Arquitectos, they consider that the position of the architect should include proposals for new ideas and themes to research and identify new directions to bioclimatic design.

The construction of buildings consumes a sixth of the world's supply of drinking water, a quarter of the timber harvesting, and three-fifths of the fossil fuels and manufactured materials. As a result, architecture has become one of the primary focuses of ecological reform.

Picciotto Arquitectos

"Today we need only observe the sad legacy of the modern movement in hostile cities around the world to see their patterns are repeated in degenerate form. While the buildings remain isolated events designed as large monumental statements to their designers, they will continue repeating mistakes again and again."

PLANTA PRIMER PISO CONJUNTO
Escala 1:125

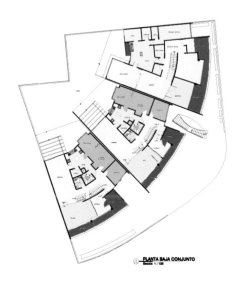

PLANTA BAJA CONJUNTO
Escala 1:125

190 Neptuno—2012
Mexico DF

This set is composed of three residential houses on three levels. These houses are provided with the features necessary for human habitat such as: generous architectural areas, shapes, and colors duly oriented, and a great efficiency in services and facilities. The general areas of this set are: lobby and access service, fitness/health center, swimming pool, multi-purpose room with kitchen, cellar, and guardhouse. The architectural program for each building is considered on three levels and a basement level. The living areas, dining room, family room, kitchen, half bath, and lobby are on the ground level. On the first level there are two bedrooms with bathrooms and dressing rooms and a full study or TV room. On the second level are a bedroom and bathroom for domestic help, as well as the master bedroom with full bathroom and dressing room.

rdlp Arquitectos consists of a team of architects with different profiles, working with external collaborations of architects, real estate engineers, and promoters, to obtain a high degree of specialization in each stage of the project. In their office, they acknowledge that architecture is generated through people's needs and an understanding of the physical, cultural, and climatic contexts. Architecture comes from a sum of elements defining a building: structure, form, context connections,

rdlp Arquitectos

materials, and its ability to convey sensations towards its users and spectators. As a team, they have a highly personalized service with which they offer a detailed approach to projects according to the specific needs. Questioning preconceptions and trying new methodologies is part of their process; reinvention, along with responsible and conscious design, regardless the project scale, complements their method of designing current architecture.

**La casa Sta. Engracia—2012
Monterrey, Nuevo Leon**

Located at the end of a closed street with one of the best views to the south, toward the Sierra Madre, the clients requested a house with a broad range of requirements, but the most clearly emphasized was how they wanted to live in the house. They needed a house that could transform and extend outward while retaining privacy from the outside. For this, rdlp Arquitectos proposed an L-shaped house that could fully open into the property.

On the outside, two large walls running through the house from side to side emphasize the L shape. These walls, besides defining spaces, separate areas of transit to other areas along the same walls.

Proposed materials are directly relevant to the extreme climate of the region. On the walls with a greater degree of sun exposure, ventilated panels were proposed. The roof garden has regional plants with low maintenance and a bed of volcanic rock that reduces solar contact.

Serrano Monjaraz Arquitectos was founded in Mexico City in 1992. Their goal is the development of architectural spaces in which quality is achieved by the correct use of the materials and light is incorporated as a creative element.

The principals, Juan Pablo Serrano Orozco and Rafael Monjaraz Fuentes, show their capability and performance in every architecture field with the support of multidisciplinary teams. A great number of their projects have received important awards in Mexico and abroad.

Serrano Monjaraz Arquitectos

Their structure and professionalism has given them the opportunity to work in association with other architecture firms and architects. They have been invited to national and international competitions and they actively participate shaping and promoting architecture.

For Serrano Monjaraz Arquitectos, architecture is their way to collaborate in the development of a better urbane context, because the correct design of the architectural spaces is the only way to create better cities. In the last twenty years, they have seen how one of the major cities in the world keeps on growing and they had the fortune to have been a part of many important changes.

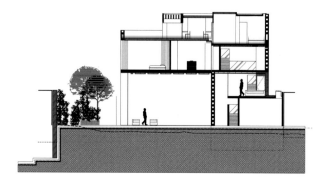

Casa Tierra—2012
Mexico DF

The construction system of Casa Tierra uses Pressed Earth Blocks (PEB) made from soil at the site. This system was selected because it is aesthetically pleasing as well as cost and energy efficient, fire and pest resistant, virtually soundproof, durable, and structurally sound. PEB provides complete architectural freedom and is made from non-toxic readily available natural raw material. Compared to other systems, it is more flexible and does not affect the width of the walls. The 90% soil from the site was pressed with 3% concrete and 7% lime.

The Pressed Earth Blocks are distributed in three different positions around the perimeter of the whole house generating box walls, both solid and hollow, with a circle hole. The distribution was done in order to use the inside part of the blocks in different ways. Some of the hollow blocks were used in the interior as well as to receive the concrete structure. Other hollow blocks were use to generate a lattice that gives a magnificent light effect to the interior of the house during sunrise and sunset. The interior walls are a single unit thick.

Taking advantage of the characteristically sunny weather of Mexico City, solar collectors were installed to heat 100% of the water necessary for the daily activities. The lighting design incorporates a central control system with low voltage lamps.

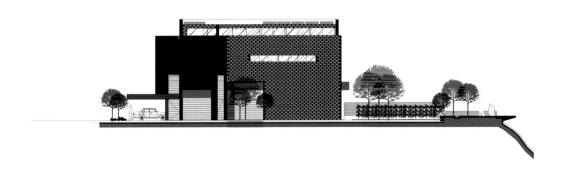

SPRB is an architecture studio directed by Laura Sánchez Penichet and Carlos Rodríguez Bernal. The departure point in their projects is always the landscape. Whether it is a natural area or an interior space, they study the relationship between constructed objects and the open spaces among them. The serious challenge of working with the "idea of the landscape" lies in its capacity to reach new dimensions, to break through the limits, to blur the silhouettes, and retrace again the familiar profiles that have been known as architecture.

SPRB

The exploration is, in different ways, of spaces other than those of architectural designs, materials other than those that architecture knows and manipulates. The places that emerge between buildings, the spaces established outside the architecture meant to contain the social activities, the soil to nurture the vegetation, are conceived as another presence in the city.

The success of an architecture tuned-in with the landscape (rather than integrated to it) lies precisely in its ability to provide technical and plastic solutions that are amazing, unusual, enriching, and never paralyzed by the presence of nature.

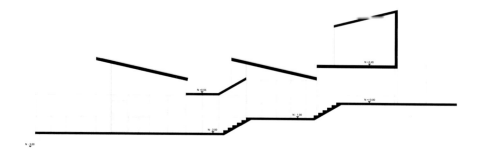

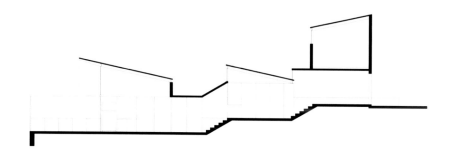

216 **Casa RB—2007**
Morelia, Michoacán

A small house with long views, a sequence of patios and pavilions with huge windows to look through, and pavements, vegetation, and, at a distance, the mountains. The topography allowed extending the limits of the house beyond its site. Not all the landscape can be walked, but all can be watched.

Since its foundation in 1991, Taller de Architectura has worked with the intention of developing a contemporary architecture sensitive to the context and the environment, combining an appropriate selection of materials from the region with the best technology available.

For architects Mauricio Rocha and partner Gabriela Carrillo, their vocation is to work with their team and create architectural projects that dignify construction. For all the team, 100% supervision of every step of the project is vital and they are very demanding in the results, both in concept and practice, as well as in the execution of the architectural details. Their more than twenty years of experience stands them out as a firm that will continue to transform the architecture of Mexico.

Taller de Arquitectura

The dignity and quality of the spaces is a constant in all the projects they do and they are always looking for the perfect balance of budget, context, typology, and of course, the final user. They are committed to architecture, therefore they create spaces that give a better quality of life for the user.

In addition to their professional activities, architects Mauricio Rocha and Gabriela Carrillo invest a significant amount of their time bringing up the new generations of architects.

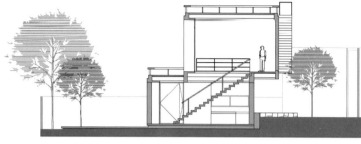

CORTE TRANSVERSAL

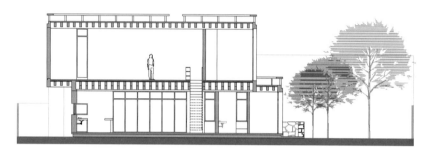

CORTE LONGITUDINAL

224 Casa Studio Oaxaca—2008
Oaxaca, Oaxaca

The Oaxaca House and Studio, built for an artist that works in plastic, is composed of two equal-sized volumes. The client's desire for a terrace for the upper floor studio inspired the architects to create two staggered volumes, one atop the other, where the roof of the lower volume would become the terrace of the second floor. The interior stair becomes the link and pivot between the two volumes.

The house is sited on an irregularly shaped lot, placed close to the shortest-length side on the terrain so as to create an expansive garden and to provide the best orientation for the north-facing studio and west-facing breakfast room. The house itself acts as a curtain protecting the terrace from the fierce late-afternoon sun and was conceived as being contained within the expansive garden that surrounds it. The principal axes of the composition leads the eye to the garden, as the interior spaces open to a large panorama of lush surroundings.

The color palette of the house plays an important role. Ochre and reds define the exteriors from the clay-tile floor and the Tezontle skin of the house to the red earth of the patio. In contrast, the interiors are of warm-toned woods and white surfaces balancing the intensity of the red-toned exterior and finding harmony with the pinks of the Bougainvillea and purples of the Jacarandas.

The structural system reinforces the concept of the two staggered volumes with roof systems of wood-beam construction where at the points the first floor supports the second, the beams double their height again emphasizing the conceptual part of the house.

A narrow exterior stair, cantilevered from the volume, connects the artist's studio with the roof terrace. On the roof terrace, the handrails become benches upon which the inhabitant can sit, admiring the view of the lush garden and the treetops, with the city of Oaxaca in the distance.

A central aim was to create a garden with a house as opposed to a house with a garden.

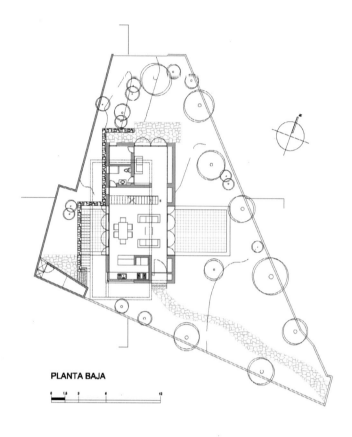

PLANTA BAJA

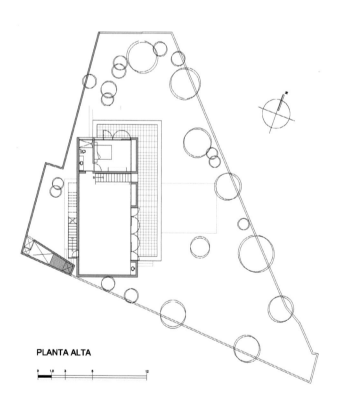

PLANTA ALTA

Immersed in cities forged of iron and concrete, where chaos is potentially profitable and the urban context resorted to formulas of construction that are devoid of creative spontaneity every day, taller5 delivers proposals that address everyday life with self-expression, freshness, dignity, and encouragement. They strive for life that flows in relationship with the space, which is not described, but is interpreted. A controversial and endless criticism by groups and individuals who

taller5 arquitectos

pigeonhole styles and trends, persecuted by passing fads and without any social impact, taller5 understands architecture as an evolution of cyclical movements in art and that it is impossible to define colors, textures, materials, or geometric formalisms as they would wish. Trying to define them would create limitations to creative representation. Taller5 arquitectos, then, refine without leaving aside historical formalisms, creating autonomous models in each architectural proposal.

232 Casa Villas—2010
Leon, Guanajuato

Nothing could be more enlightening than the concept taller5 applied in the Casa Villas: its exceptional location and orientation is defined by a space bounded by a large terrace, a swimming pool, and its access, in ascending order.

The house runs, to a large extent, horizontally, in such a way that the journey takes on the "*galerón*" (a double height space and very long) in the social area and the intimate volume of the private area's two levels. It is in this intimate area of the house, which contains the view within the terrace, that a fireplace wall rises in parallel to the reference of the higher social area.

7XA Arquitectura understands the city as something constantly in formation and dissolution, transformed by the wills of its many citizens. Architecture is an essential part of this transformational process. When the firm is allowed to work with the city, they think of being in a moment in time, where the environment is neither precise nor fixed. 7XA arquitectura respond to less than specific contexts, to contexts that are changing as they follow the urban vitality. Given this fact, 7XA conducts a tireless search for the perfectible through the continuous redefinition of its design process (7 = perfection, X = research, A = architecture).

For them, architecture is more than a profession, it is a passion—a passion between art and science, between creation and rational knowledge. The passion leads the way, but rationality provides the substance. Building is also their passion, but it doesn't exist without the understanding of why and for what they are building. Every situation for them is in a particular space and time. Their architecture is born from observation and meticulous study at the site; its configuration and their senses provide the context.

7XA Arquitectura

For 7XA, the interior space is designed to create meaning. It should provide intimacy, without being heavy or mandatorily massive. It should be fluid and flexible. It uses light in different ways: natural light is hygienic, as the "moderns" proposed; artificial light creates interior effects.

In developing domestic space, they look for a neutral and flexible architecture that allows the home to be adapted to the changing conditions of contemporary life. Within these parameters, they seek an architecture that is adequate for changes in fashion without requiring change to the structure itself. The spaces are perceived as having more amplitude and relief. All of these are intended to generate maximum comfort.

They seek an architecture for the time in which they live, generating living buildings that resolve every point architecturally and offer the client spaces that go far beyond what he could imagine. Every building represents a unique challenge. Each project generates a very special link between client and architect. The decisions made together must be a perfect balance between estimates, architectural plasticity, and functionality in every sense.

PLANTA ALTA
11. ESTANCIA FAMILIAR
12. RECÁMARA PRINCIPAL
13. RECÁMARA 2
14. RECÁMARA 3

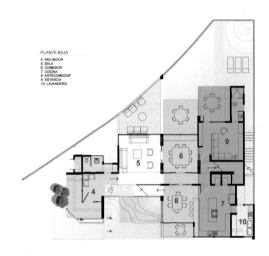

PLANTA BAJA
4. RECIBIDOR
5. SALA
6. COMEDOR
7. COCINA
8. ANTECOMEDOR
9. ESTANCIA
10. LAVANDERIA

242 **CANTIZAL HOUSE—2008**
Santa Catarina, Nuevo Leon

The house is located on an irregular property with the best view facing north. It is a sequence of spaces that goes from the public to the private. The house acts as an architectural promenade. All of these spaces are related to the exterior. The rooms facing north are those that required sunlight, while the rooms facing south need privacy.

Walking through the garden in front of the property at the narrow corner, the land and the house become an open space until the path ends. There is a stairs here that raise up to the second floor. At this point, the same promenade heads in the opposite direction. Small spaces downstairs are able to transform public into private, or, when combined, form a big social area.

A long hall, naturally illuminated, on the second floor, organizes the bedrooms that, depending in their location, face views of La Sierra Madre or el Cerro de las Mitras, and reach ventilated and illuminated spaces. There is a multipurpose room where the second floor begins. This is a place where kids can socialize and do the school work. A bridge connects to the bedrooms, separating the spaces and creating privacy.

Analyzing views, working with the site's natural conditions, creating spaces that go from public to private, make the house an amazing composition of plans, volumes, solids, and gaps along the land.

15   Adan Lozano Arquitectos

Rio Amazonas III ote.
Col. del Valle
66220 Garza Garcia, NL
+52 818 356 0315
adanlozano@prodigy.net.mx
www.adanlozano@terra.com.mx
Contact: Architect Adan Lozano

23   Agraz Arquitectos

San Felipe 872
Col. Jesus Chapel
44200 Guadalajara, Jal
+52 333 827 4500
taller@agrazarquitectos.com
www.agrazarquitectos.com
Contact: Architect Ana Guerreosantos

Architect Directory

33   Alejandro Herrasti Arquitectos

Av. Mexico 99 PH-C
Col. Hipodromo Condesa
06140 Mexico DF
alejandroherrasti@prodigy.net.mx
www.alejandroherrasti.com
Contact: Alejandro Herrasti

43   Archetonic, S.A. de C.V.

Bosque de Ciruelos No. 130-404
Col. Miguel Hidalgo
11700 Mexico DF
+52 555 596 76771
info@archetonic.com.mx
www.archetonic.com.mx
Contact: Architect Jacobo Micha Mizrahi

250

145 JSª Arquitectos

Culican 123, piso 6 y 7
Col. Condesa
06170 Mexico DF
+52 551 085 9924
info@jsa.com.mx
www.jsa.com.mx
Contact: Architect Javier Sanchez

155 Kababie Arquitectos

Edgar Allan Poe 326A
Col. Polanco
11550 Mexico DF
+52 555 280 6679
elias@kababiearquitectos.com
http://www.kababiearquitectos.com
Contact: Architect Elias Kababie

165 LEAP Laboratorio en Arquitectura Progresiva

José María Heredia 2405
Col. Providencia
44657 Guadalajara, Jal
+52 33 3630 6028
raul@leap.com.mx
heriberto@leap.mx
www.leap.mx
Contact: Architect Raúl Juárez or Heriberto Hernández

251

175 López Duplan Arquitectos

Mayorga 121 PB
Col. Lomas de Virreyes
11000 Mexico DF
+52 555 596 3452
lda@duplan.com.mx
http://duplan.com.mx
Contact: Architect Claudia López Duplan

215   SPRB

Colonias 221, Penthouse
Col. Americana
44160 Guadalajara, Jal
+52 333 825 8713
Info@sprb.net
www.sprb.net
Contact: Architect Laura Sanchez/Carlos Rodriguez Bernal

223   Taller de Arquitectura
(Mauricio Rocha + Gabriela Carrillo)

Miguel Ángel de Quevedo 95
Col. Chimalistac
01070 Mexico DF
ı 52 555 661 2120
info@tallerdearquitectura.com.mx
http://www.tallerdearquitectura.com.mx/
Contact: Architect Mauricio Rocha Iturbide

231   taller5 arquitectos

Luis Lozano #309 altos.
Col. Panorama.
37160 León, Gto
+52 477 718 5477
taller5@taller5.com.mx
www.taller5.com.mx
Contact: Architect Octavio Arreola Calleros

241   7XA Arquitectura

+52 818 358 2900
informacion@7xa.com.mx
www.7xa.com.mx
Contact: Architect Carlos Ortiz

254 *Photographer Index*

Barragán, The Complete Works. New York: Princeton Architectural Press, 1996.

de Haro, Fernando and Omar Fuentes. *Arquitectos Mexicanos, Una Visipn Contemporanea.* México D.F.: Arquitectos Mexicanos Editores S.A. de C.V., 2004.

_____. *Mexican Interiors: Style & Personality.* México D.F.: Arquitectos Mexicanos Editores S.A. de C.V., 2003.

Levick, Melba and Gina Hyams. *Mexicasa, The Enchanting Inns and Haciendas of Mexico.* San Francisco: Chronicle Books, 2001.

_____. *In a Mexican Garden: Courtyards, Pools, and Open-Air Living Rooms.* San Francisco: Chronicle Books, 2005.

Legorreta, Ricardo & Victor Legorreta. *LEGORRETA + LEGORRETA: New Buildings & Projects: 1997–2003.* New York: Rizzoli, 2004.

Levick, Melba, Tony Cohan, and Masako Takahashi. *Mexicolor: The Spirit of Mexican Design.* San Francisco: Chronicle Books, 1998.

Luscombe-Whyte, Mark and Dominic Bradbury. *Mexico Architecture, Interiors & Design.* New York: Harper Collins Publishers, 2004.

Stoeltie, Barbara and Rene Stoeltie. *Living in Mexico: Vivre au Mexique.* Cologne: Taschen, 2004.

Streeter-Porter, Tim. *Casa Mexicana: The Architecture, Design and Style of Mexico.* New York: Stewart, Tabori & Chang, 1994.

_____. Streeter-Porter, Tim, and Annie Kelly. *Casa Mexicana Style.* New York: Stewart, Tabori & Chang, 2006.

Villela, Khristaan, Ellen Bradbury, and Logan Wagner. *Contemporary Mexican Design and Architecture.* Layton, Utah: GibbsSmith, Publisher, 2002.

Yampolsky, Mariana and Chloe Sayer. *The Traditional Architecture of Mexico.* New York: Thames and Hudson, 1993.

Ypma, Herbert. *Mexican Contemporary.* New York: Stewart, Tabori & Chang, 1997.

Working on this book has been a joyful and pleasurable experience, mostly because of the new friends and acquaintances I was fortunate to meet along the way. I visited architects in several cities, including Guadalajara, Monterrey, and Mexico City, and came away in awe with an appreciation for what the Mexican architects are achieving both in Mexico and around the world.

No book is ever done completely by the author without the help of others. My special thanks to Barbara Guyton, who traveled with me, interviewing all the architects, and helped with my lack of Spanish whenever the need arose, and it happened most of the time.

256 *Acknowledgments*

Thanks goes to my editors at Schiffer Publishing, Ltd., Nancy Schiffer, Jesse Marth, and Doug Congdon-Martin. without whom, and with their patience and foresight, this book may not have made it into your hands.

And finally, a great big thank you to the 26 participating architects, some who allowed me into their homes and who provided most of the photographs that you find within these pages.

I thank you all.